~~I HAVE NEVER WANTED~~ ANOTHER LIFE

Frances Klein

Riot in Your Throat
publishing fierce, feminist poetry

Klein, Frances.
1st edition.
ISBN: 979-8-9889898-5-1

Cover Art: Caleb Minear (unsplash.com)
Cover Design: Kirsten Birst
Book Design: Shanna Compton
Author Photo: Katie Doyle

Riot in Your Throat
Arlington, VA
www.riotinyourthroat.com

"I have never wanted another life, but I know the story of pursuit"
—Terrance Hayes, "Root"

"All the lives I might have had: this one, oh, this one"
—Marianne Boruch, "February"

CONTENTS

RESUME

after Michael Torres' "Down II"

I put in two years at the jack-o'-lantern factory,
awarded nose-hole-cutter of the month
ten months running. I priced freight at a drugstore
where cruise ship workers bought instant noodles
by the pallet. I was Head Assistant to a reverse
pest removal expert, working overtime putting bats
and raccoons back in attics, coaxing opossums
and skunks back under crawl spaces.
For a long time I've been angry.
One summer I was a living mandala,
folding T-shirts all day on one side of a table
while tourists unfolded them on the other.
If beauty is impermanence, my table and I
were the most beautiful couple the dock had ever seen.
I was a museum docent for a culture not my own,
telling stolen stories while the totems listened in.
I was a photo model for an illustrated pain scale,
making every face from 1 to 10,
no acting required. I was an apprentice librarian,
new to Dewey's ways. Once I went on vacation—
so my coworkers say—working from home
for a seven-pound boss, on call as a living buffet
all hours of the day and night.
Then I was a professional bathroom poet,
hired by the coolest bars and coffee shops
to cover low-lit stalls in clean limericks
for obscene prices. I have frequently been
a complication, a wrench in the spokes.
I was an AM DJ, spinning theories into facts
after midnight, giving equal airtime to Sasquatch

truthers and moon-landing deniers. I keep applying
for a position at the All Better Business Bureau,
any opening, any department: Miraculously Healed,
Finally Over It; I even put in for an entry-level spot
in Road to Recovery. I leveraged every relationship,
networked my ass off, called in every favor.
All my resumes bounced back, the rejections kind
but dismissive: you'll be a great candidate, they say,
once you get some experience.

ORIGIN STORIES

Being alive on this planet
means acknowledging that all things
were once something else.

That sponge absorbing water on the bar
was once spruce, once larch,
once hemlock, all pulped and compressed,
painted to stand out on the supermarket shelf.

Each pane of glass dividing
loved one from longed-for one—
whether high risk or long sentence—
is a composite product.
Countless grains of sand
married ancient limestone and ash
at high heat, modifying at the molecular level
to birth the see-through sheen we expect.

Before you woke up and went to sleep
and filled the hours in between
with emails and haircuts and five-dollar coffees,
you were an egg sleeping in your follicle.

Before you were an egg sleeping in your follicle,
you were the factors pushing your parents to collide:
Prince baby-talking his way through "Kiss,"
the smell of the bonfire on that hot summer night
with three bright stars in the sky.
You were fortune and pheromones
and those three stars aligning.

Or you were patience and planning,
nurses and procedures
and needle upon needle upon needle
compelling you into being.

Even the words we spend
with no thought for the cost
were once something else.
Each casual goodbye the fruit of a phrase,
God be with ye,
tree pruned and grafted
into the least committal of all departures.
A weakened branch unable to bear
the weight of its meaning.

Sponge mopping up the farewell
between mouth and teeth.
Father and son palm to palm,
pressing one more layer
of heat into the glass.

Your parent started saying goodbye to you
the moment you sparked,
each conscientious vitamin,
each placental pump of blood,
each heave of nausea
peaking in a slight wave, a turned back,
a receding into the distance.

SCHOENBAR ROAD

Freezing rain, branches rebelling
against sky to bow earthward, and the wind
spread like a sheet on a new-made bed.

Love drove us out, sled-laden: love of
speed, of icicles snapped from gutters,
their iron tint filming our tongues, love of our
father and his love of an empty kitchen.

Hill where margin trades places
with center; top and bottom both safe as
stationary, between stretches treacherous
with rise, lilt, cadence of chance and reflex.

Street sleeping dormant under winter, save
places where it roused and kicked covers
just enough, flint-thin asphalt bones exposed.

Dangling from brother's coattails, stepping in snow
where his boots have been, feet too small
to fill prints, head swiveling to breathe in

puffs of stories spilling out. We posed
on the crest as if framed, then fell to earth,
vessels off the edge of the world, and here
is where memory goes hazy, mixed with fable:

he says the street roused long enough to reach out
one long, bony finger. He says I, neither lucky
nor careful, chin-kissed curb, added red confetti

to falling flakes, ended the outing. I say smooth
skin without scar, I say green sled over blue-white snow
all day into evening, and again, again, again.

ALL THE TASKS WE GIVE THE YOUNG

*I was maybe five or six years old and the most I could have done
was let [grandma] fall on me if she decided to fall.* —Bill Withers

mist slicks the stone steps slug
trail thick lays limp along the
blueberry branches beds down
      in the moss my mother pulls me
      aside tells me to walk behind
      going up in front going down
            make of my body an offering
            to the gods of longevity   make
            of   myself   a   pillow
                  to cushion fragile bones from
                  the kiss of stone block the
                  blow make the sauce set
                        the table with the fine silver
                        held so tightly the pattern leaves
                        lines on the pad of my thumb

BETWEEN THE DEVIL AND THE CLEAR BLUE SKY

In the Tongass we had ten months a year
of the good stuff, storm clouds that would stoop, black-
berry heavy, to lick the walls of the Inside Passage.
At times it came even from an empty sky,
perspiration needling earthward from some source
beyond perception. The kids who lived out
at Mud Bight in the shanty houses built on pilings
used to call that rain "the devil beating his wife,"
the sound of it some precipitous thing
we didn't yet know, standing then on the cliff
edge of childhood before we dove over.

AT THE MIDDLE SCHOOL DANCE, ALL THE BOYS
CIRCLE UP FOR THE CRIP WALK

Their shirts are blue and red,
striped and checked, the collars popped,
armpit seams untouched by antiperspirant.

They are puppy-limbed and -footed,
eyes wide and unshuttered as lighthouses.

The music doesn't matter:
Backstreet Boys, Bloodhound Gang,
radio-edit Eminem, an arrhythmic heart-skip
of censored somethings.

The boys take turns careening across the circle,
hips loose, ankles floppy, knees jerking in and out.

None of them know enough
to try and spell anything, their moves
a scribbled mess across center court.

Here on this island, far from
everything, they know nothing
of affiliation, of territory,
of acting lookout on an LA street
while hot wind sparks a cigarette butt
still smoldering in the gutter.

In the flash of a single-colored strobe,
their teeth are blue, then purple, then blue again.
They laugh and hoot, jeer and clap
as they each in turn shrug on so easily

the soft-elbowed coat
of taking something not their own
and wearing it lightly.

THEY TELL ME I'M GONNA BE A HEARTBREAKER ONE DAY
an erasure of Barbara Kingsolver's "The Poisonwood Bible"

Boys

                take   immediately to

The prison

           of   my skin

                             white   and
                                           remote

formal charges have been filed,

       and the most likely sentence will be life

though there are other possibilities.

      (I have no idea how to be kind to myself.

          Living

              seems unkind beyond belief.)

VENMO REQUEST FOR THERAPY MONEY FROM THE BOY WHO CALLED ME AN "8" IN HIS MYSPACE HOTNESS RANKINGS

For the way my lizard brain craved those last two points

For the way I scoured the rankings for my name

For the way I started at the bottom

For the way my heart was in the basement
  knowing that the only thing worse than a low ranking was no ranking

For the way I didn't even blink when I saw that Tiffany's ass was a 7
  but her face was a 3

For the way countless men and women worked long hours
  missing golden anniversaries and oboe solos with only one wrong note
  to string together the ones and zeros of the world wide web
  for our education and enlightenment

For the way we can find each other across time and space
  use the magic of the internet for anything we choose

and we use it to destroy each other

I REWATCH MY EXES' FAVORITE FILMS AND IMAGINE OUR LIVES TOGETHER

J—

an erasure of The Empire Strikes Back

You worship

    nothing but

        danger

        and

    a good story. I think you

can't be   both   gorgeous

    and vulnerable

At   night   together

    you

        look at me   like

a shelter   covered with snow

    but   in

        plain day

you

    move past   my

        smoldering ruins

E—

a cento of the Derek Jarman film Blue

Once there are only two of us, you set to work mapping the solemn geography of human limits. You are slow and deliberate, a dedicated cartographer.

•

The empty book of a new year opens.

I am the marble, you the sculptor. Your tool is a refined meanness, carving away anything in me that does not reflect you.

•

Another year passes.

It's not so bad, this melting of self. This slow drip, minute by minute, into the river of hours that leads to your sea.

I submerge in you and come up half dissolved.

•

Each day is a room where I sit waiting to hear what parts of me have been lost in the night. I clasp my hands before me. When I part them, they disappear.

If I lose half myself, will my self be halved?

•

Your frustration: after all this time, you have not found the core of me. You describe it: a naked lightbulb in a dark and ruined room.

You try to enter me like a virus, but I am out of your reach. I am walking behind the sky.

F—

after Planet of the Apes *(1968)*

Beloved,

When I saw you there
on your knees before me,
Heston prone in the sand
before the Statue of Liberty,
I knew what it was
to be a fallen idol.

I am crowned with stone
certainty, beloved. When I left you
I did so early, mourning
nothing but the life
we might have had.

I rub the rust of regret
from my skin. I keep
my joints limber, my head
on a swivel. I will not say
I am looking back toward you, beloved,
but I will not say I am not.

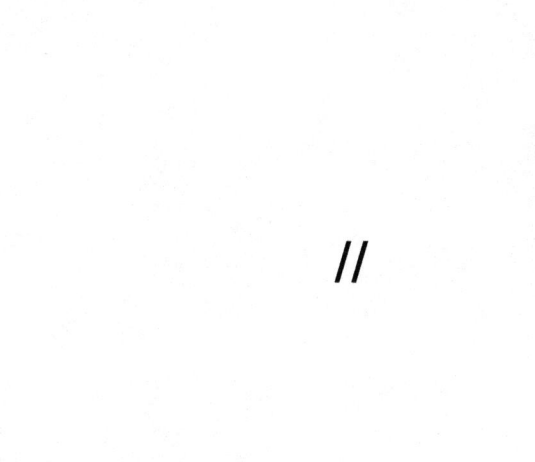

TARGETED

They are interspersed among
the staged-candid shots
and artfully lit sushi plates—
clothing ads where bow-bellied women
place protective hands on the bump,
hospital video spots where a squalling newborn
is laid on his stunned father's chest—
all your views and purchases and split-second
pauses while scrolling have red-ringed
a target around your open wound.

Negative pregnancy tests clutter the bin
and suddenly the internet is a minefield—
you tread carefully through vacation photos
to the left, girls' nights to the right,
but one wrong step triggers a diaper ad,
a dimpled little guy, all brown eyes and curls,
and the aftermath of the detonation is less
like having the wind knocked out of you,
more like scanning the tree line
to see where your lungs landed.

People tell you, patly, to get off
social media, so you do, but the rest
of the internet is still out there,
and these days you can't opt out
of online, so maybe the day
is going fine—your students are working
and chatting and singing along
with Totally '90s Pandora,

but there's a sniper on the roof—
the ad break is coos and gurgles
and *Protect the skin you love most*
with Eucerin and you can't
breathe and you can't
leave and you can't remember
what the kid just asked you
so they repeat it then repeat it again,
and the rest of the day is hazy
while you keep pressure
on the bleeding.

Bit by bit you build your camouflage,
change your gender on every account
you can think of, decline all cookies,
browse incognito, leave
your phone in the car
when you have to buy anything
that might read as feminine
(the list is a mystery—
tampons, of course, or makeup, but
paper towels? Tangerines? Triple A batteries?).
You open Playboy and ESPN
on three different devices
and scroll while you watch TV,
constructing an impenetrable carapace.
Now when the shots are fired,
they go wide, watches and Wranglers,
dick pills and protein powder.

Eventually, the internet is an escape
once again from the crack shots

and stray grenades of the real world.
And are you happy? Of course not.
And are you safe? Of course not,
no one promised any of those things
to anyone in life. All you can do
is harden the target.

OTHER PEOPLE'S PREGNANCY ANNOUNCEMENTS

Potted plants
on the windowsill
watch hard rain soak
everything green
that's free.

ESTRADIOL THE MIMIC

*Estradiol, like many fertility drugs, induces side effects that
mimic the symptoms people often feel in early pregnancy.*

Like the Milk Snake, robed
in lapping bands of sandstone, salt,
and sable to imitate its cousin Coral,
hiding in plain sight from the hawks
and skunks that would make it a meal.

Like the Walking Stick, segmented
length blending with the detritus of the forest
floor to offer shelter from the curious birds
and rodents who might spy its movements
and know it to be more than wind.

Like the Robber Fly, camouflaged assassin,
robed in marigold and shade, coiled behind
the flower petals to catch anything
that moves, be it beetle, lacewing, butterfly;
no mercy even for its own cousins.

Like the Death's Head Hawkmoth,
which perfumes itself with the scent
of the bees it robs, waved on
by the hive guards to the inner sanctum
where it feasts without reproach.

All of this mimicry a drive for survival,
for safety, for sustenance, for one
more moment on this earth. From what,
then, do the chemicals flooding my
body think they are saving me?

BAD THERAPIST SAYS

can I pray for you / you look so pretty today / remind me what you said last week / I lost my notes / if you're able to work every day, it's not depression / anxiety is all in the mind / none of it is real / none of it is realistic / why are you scared of a death not your own / aren't we all striving for heaven / you are a serious case / come every week / bring your credit card / I'll pray for you tonight / you're too smart to be a teacher / you should quit your job / you could do real work elsewhere / I have a reputation for being able to speak for God / I can see why everyone likes you / your negative attitude is why the procedures aren't working / I wasn't excited for my own pregnancy / the baby died / birth defects / sometimes I wonder if I caused them / my attitude, my lack of surrender / do you think it was me / I'll pray about it tonight, when I pray for you / I feel like I can tell you anything / your voice is so pleasing / you should have a podcast / or be in movies / or on tv / you should stop the procedures / it doesn't seem natural / I pray for you every night / God told me you would have twins / I'm thinking of starting a new career / wellness coaching / or life coaching / or traveling the world / you never told me that / not in every session / not at all / I don't suggest stopping treatment / God brought you here for a reason / God does this to you for a reason / can you write a review for my website / a good one / that says how much I helped you

"IN THE BOWER / THE ROSES HANG SO HEAVY—"

I am depressed, and—

Wait. A poem can't just say "I am depressed."
The poem has to be coy and oblique.
For God's sake, it has to be *literary*.

The reader should leave the poem
wondering if it is about depression.
They should say to a friend, "Here, read this poem
about depression," and have the friend disagree,
since the poem seems to be much more about two fish,
or a diner going out of business, or Spanx.

The poem should be cutting, incisive.
It should expose the ugly underbelly of society.
Yet the poem should also be beautiful, should describe
leaning against the cool glass of the car window
tracing the path of a lone raindrop.
The chill condensation should be crafted
with such crystalline clarity that the reader
is left thinking that depression can't be all that bad
if a depressed person can write a poem like that.

For contrast, the poem about depression
should have lots of light in it.
Early morning light, midday light,
anything except the waning twilight of evening,
which is too on the nose.

In a pinch, the poem about depression can go outside,
although it doesn't really feel up to it.

The poem can gather plants for its metaphors,
can braid a crown of ivy for the green it lends
to the lines the poem has about envy,
about lying motionless on the lawn
while the grass grows around it.

Ideally, the poem will also include one devastating stanza
about a bower of white roses,
although it doesn't know where it will find one
and the botanical garden closes early on Sundays
and getting there means pants and glasses and keys
and oh God it's so much simpler to just put on *Grey's Anatomy*
and write about the bower later, maybe.

When the poem about depression ends,
it should be on a hopeful note
because no one likes a whiner.
The poem should end at sunrise
or on a new budding branch
or a bacterial culture persevering
on the dishes in the sink
that should have been washed a week ago.

By no means should the poem simply end
by refusing to change its bra
and taking the whole sleeve
of Oreos to bed,
but it will anyway.

EVERYTHING NOT SAVED WILL BE LOST

a grief symphony with thanks to the Nintendo Corporation

First Movement

Before

While I was waiting for you, everything

I wrote was an elegy for a thing I had not

yet lost. I slung my grieving grudge over my shoulder, saved

my smiles for those like me who survived by sheer will,

maintained by the cirrus-thin dream that someday we, too, could be

grieving something real, only happy once you existed to be lost.

Before

The endless scroll shows me everything

I want in the hands of others. So as not

to seem bitter, I place a robin's egg saved

from the gutter back in its nest, will

myself to like the photos of ultrasounds that have be-

come my whole feed. I am on the sidelines of a game I have not played, yet
   already forfeited.

6 weeks, 7 days

Once you are conceived, I lose everything
singular about myself, everything not
plural, not compound-noun. I am saved
from the still pond of my mind by the ripple-will
of our body that pulls what is needed for you to be.
Everything is used; nothing is wasted.

24 weeks, 2 days

We swear we will remember everything:
the tornado-yellow sky in early afternoon, the not-
quite kicks against our palms, the money saved
when nothing but Campbell's will
stay down. We want a road map to be
preserved for future journeys. Next time, we swear, we will not get lost.

5 / 20 / 19, 5:33 PM

my everything-

hoarding heart unravels, I will not

be saved

from myself, my will

to fall into this new us, to be,

even to myself, estranged

2 months

Once you are here, I take pictures of everything,

every cochlear curl, every clenched fist like a blush-rose not

yet bloomed, every way you saved

me. I fill albums with proof of your existence, as if this will

delay by even a minute the day when you will be

so far from me that photos are the only way to show what I have lost.

4 months

There are days when I am tired of everything.

Days when, by nightfall, I have not

gone a second without being touched, my sanity only saved

by considering you an extension of myself, and even that takes all my will-

power. We are an unspeakable assemblage of limbs, something that cannot be

solitary. On the day we separate, I will be lost.

2 years

We want more of this everything,

to be a garden so soaked, not

a single earthworm remains underground. We think we will be saved

from the pain of drought by our already blooming beds, will

till, plant, harvest with ease. How could we know we would be

thirteen months without rain? How can we count all this nothing?

PREGNANCY TRACKER

This week, your baby is a lemon the size of a golf ball. A Boeing 747 the size of a hummingbird. Your baby is a blue whale the size of a bait herring. A neon sign the size of a light socket. A two-hundred-year-old oak the size of an acorn. Your baby is an old-growth forest the size of the preservation society's budget. A forty-hour workweek the length of a single evening. This week your baby is a multihour, cross-department meeting the size of an "out of office" message. A time zone the size of a wristwatch. A library the size of a zip file. A body of work the size of a single pull quote. Your baby is an ever expanding, unboundaried universe the size of a postage stamp. Limitless potential the size of realized talent. An 8-lane freeway the size of the life in the rearview mirror.

DEAR SON,

I woke up possessed.
I redefined self.
How fine, I thought,
this sweet-wild waking.

The difference is you,
face to face, but as distant
from me as ever.

Your gift, the one
that will not waver:

You never truly leave,
you pour through me
like a river.

BORN IN THE RAIN

I was born in the rain, pearls of perspiration
embroidering the wavetops.

My husband was born in a deluge
that washed out the shortcut
his father took to the hospital,
my mother-in-law torn by back labor,
heart flooded with fear and unshed love.

Our son is a miscible liquid,
both the estuary of our mingled waters
and his own unknowable storm.

The sky opened on his life
the moment we stepped out into it,
droplets limning his lashes
while I waited on the curb
feeling fraudulent and grateful,
unaware of the pain to come.

His eyes are the color
of a slow, silt-soaked river:
muddy Missouri, Mississippi molasses.

On my first birthday as a mother,
I swaddle him on the porch swing as rain
shakes the branches, his Mississippi eyes
darting back and forth with the birds
that are bending the air between trees.

The morning I was born, my mother
gazed out the hospital window
to see rain streaking the streetlights
before returning to the vernix-streaked
window of my face.

SUDDEN UNDERTOW

after Joshua Bennett

Spring paused to catch its breath
and I was gone, swept out to sea
by you, sudden undertow.

When I finally came up for air
and took inventory of what remained
of me, all I had were legs

to tread water, no land in sight.
I did not know that in the depths
beneath me loomed my leviathan

new life, mouth agape, ready
to consume me. Then everything inverted
and I was the shore you washed up on.

I watched you unbuckling your mouth,
waited for the strobe pulse
of your scream, but instead you gave

three sighs, an elliptical entry
into life, and I knew what it meant
to be wholly for another—

to become a hometown,
the aperture through which
you come into this life,

bringing with you
a whole populace in one body,
peopling my avenues.

DUPLEX: HOUSE OF JOY

after Jericho Brown

The sun finds me awake when it rises,
your eyes watching me from behind the curve of my breast.

    The curve of my breast, your eyes,
    the sun, all round like the wheel of time that brought us together.

Our time together has been short
and mostly sleepless, nights I lie awake.

    I lie awake at night fearing any falter in your breath,
    sentinel-ready to sooth your chill, your hunger.

Mostly I am a sentinel uncalled,
the texture of your breath constant.

    Your constant breath, the rasp of sandpaper on wood,
    soothes me to sleep as if I was the child, not you.

If I was the child, I would rouse you before dawn,
let the sun find us awake when it rises—

SELF-PORTRAIT WITH BREAST PUMP

Latch

    Beneath my skin, mammary glands unfold
    like a child's drawing of a daisy—
    fat, bulbous petals arrayed around a pointed center,
    plumped lobules jostling for position.

Unlatch

    I go around my whole life unmindful
    of the fluids moving through veins, arteries, glands, ducts
    until suddenly it is possible to set a watch
    by the swelling of the incoming tide.

Latch

    In these moments, I am an assemblage
    of disconnected limbs, in the foreground the breast,
    the lap, the crook of the arm—
    the rest of me a slow dissolve in the background.

Unlatch

    It is no longer possible to distinguish between myself
    and the machine that goes everywhere with me,
    fluted attachments protruding, tubes tangling,
    the whole scope of my world bound by a cord's length.

Latch

My whole life I try to be solid, present, a fixed point.
Then, in one interminable instant, the flower blooms,
the machine whirs, the body dissolves.
In an instant, there is only the incoming tide.

if i do not complete the thought you will never
after Amy Miller

the car barreling through the yellow light will not

your spine will not snap like a greenstick when you jump from the

no need to throw myself into the canal to keep water from clogging

the hunk of hot dog won't lodge in your

allergens closing your throat as you

the fever torching the forests of your cheeks will not

thick smoke replacing the air in each room of the house until

tornado whipping away the roof, debris closing us in with no

the silence from your room does not mean

all day i static-stop thoughts that might

for i am determined that you will always

BIRD WATCHING

It was just that time of summer where your life
smarts and itches, and the bottle blue flies are huge
as your thumb knuckle.

Each restless night fades to restless day where you stalk down
the to-do list all morning, mope from laundry to dinner to dishes
all afternoon. And nothing you do is what you want to be doing

because there is nothing in life you want to do, at least not in this life, the one
where you buy stamps, get your oil changed, where you try to meet deadlines
while your child puts one wet finger in your ear to mark his territory.

Photos show you far-flung lives outside this one with mountains
and oceans, lives with gardens in bloom and wave-rocked docks
and sunset-colored cocktails and your skin itches until you want to molt

the whole of it and step, baby snake smooth into the Pacific, drink in hand.
But then there is a blue jay out your window, one eye cocked to take in your life,
even the parts you have stopped seeing.

The jay is bluer than the flies, closer than the ocean,
blue soothing the bone-itch of this life for the moment
between landing and takeoff.

EVERYTHING NOT SAVED WILL BE LOST

a grief symphony with thanks to the Nintendo Corporation

Second Movement

6 weeks, 1 day

This joy, when I am handed everything

I want, feels spun-glass fragile. I should not

grip too tightly, like this bauble of elation I saved

and scrimped for will

shatter at the merest pressure, can be

blown away by the faintest breath, so easily broken.

6 weeks, 2 days

You will have everything

we bought for your brother, not

a cloth or toy wasted. We saved

it all in the attic and garage, a monument to our hopes. We will

need to find more space, we say, be

more careful so that nothing precious is lost.

6 weeks, 5 days

I buy out the bookstore, everything

they have about big brothers, new babies, not

a coherent thought, just the bubbling over of hope saved

simmering for years on the back burner. I will

myself to ignore the smoke alarm blaring in my body, will not be

discouraged by this warning of what might be lost.

8 weeks, 1 day

The nurse's face says everything

the doctor will not.

We will not be saved

from the drain-pull will

of a body determined to be

gone.

———

i tried everything

    you could not

        be saved

in what new ways will

    i be

        lost

8 weeks, 4 days

In the bookstore I wear an oversized pad to collect everything

that was supposed to be your body. I can not

pull my eyes from the children's books, those blank lines saved

for children to write their names in, as you never will.

I am swaddling you drip by drip, contraction by contraction, to be

buried with trash. I make your shape with my empty hands to show what I
    have lost.

After

I had everything

planned, opening gambit to final checkmate. I did not

anticipate this opponent, saved

no pieces for protection. What will

your next move be,

I am asked, but I know the game is over.

BLIGHTED OVUM

an erasure of Barbara Kingsolver's The Poisonwood Bible

bad luck:

the smoke
the mosquitoes

The   pitch-dark   night   the pounding rain

My mind ached like a broken bone
as I struggled to stand in the new place I found myself.

I'd walked   my whole life,

and now without warning my body had fallen

where I   couldn't follow

Out of the thunderous rain the
clear   voice:

rage

THE DEATH OF THE DREAM

a golden shovel with thanks to Rainer Maria Rilke and Captain America

I ran over a squirrel today, in the daylight. I almost
stopped. On the other side of the comic shop, two men are talking everything
guns—their weight and caliber, their one round eye always dead serious
about winning the staring contest. The day I buy sunscreen is
always the day it rains the hardest. It's difficult,
now, to put a finger on the day's lowest moment: the men and
their portable reapers, the impotence of my sunscreen as the rain soaks
    everything,
the double bump of the squirrel beneath the wheels. Maybe it is
this: when everything is serious, nothing is serious.

These low hours lay bare the truth that scrapes under everything like a hair
    shirt—if
Captain America can be killed, so can you.

I ASK MY THERAPIST WHERE THE SADNESS GOES

She says, picture a box. Every detail.
Picture it airtight, its intricate lid
sighing into place without a whisper.
Picture a ball of light the size of a
marble. Make it whatever color says
sadness: azure, amethyst, army green.
Picture yourself tipping your palm. Picture
the light dimming as the lid on the box
clicks home. Put the box on a shelf. Close the
door to the room where the shelf and the box
and the light in the box are kept. Lock it.
Never open it again. Leave the key
in a house in another state. I still
feel sad, I say. Oh yes, she says. Always.

WHAT ARRIVES ON YOUR DUE DATE

Here is a leaf, sun-dappled,
still latched to the branch.

Here is a butterfly, fresh from the creche,
too toddler-fingered to fly.

Here is a squirrel, all rust and brush, gnawing
its way through your jack-o'-lantern's sinuses.

Here is the snow globe of memory with your aunt inside,
one hand holds a geode, the other a hammer.

Here is the nail the hammer was missing,
picking the teeth of your vacuum.

Here is nothing you asked for: an unraveled hem,
a swarm of millipedes, six stitches above the thicket of your brow.

Here is a shade of blue that has a name
only in certain dead languages.

Here is the living language of loss
to coax open your jaw, place on your tongue

the future, that bitter pill, to massage
your throat until you swallow.

TWINS

There are two skeletons arranged side by side
on the laminated place mat.

One was printed by the teacher,
one drawn by my son.

They are Schwarzenegger-and-DeVito style twins.
One is executed in clear, crisp lines,

the other is wobbly, one-eyed,
an upside-down smile drooping at the corner.

These are my two children:
the one who lives forever

in the mind, perfect template,
and his brother, who must live

in this busy, terrible, wonderful,
bone-bruising world.

WINTER AWAITING SPRING

an erasure of Stephen King's The Colorado Kid

when the fog rolled in and the entire   world

seemed to be canceled   the foghorn

voice of some ancient beast

told her

living has a way of creeping into your blood

she   found
          a new

life   pretty much interchangeable with any

of the others

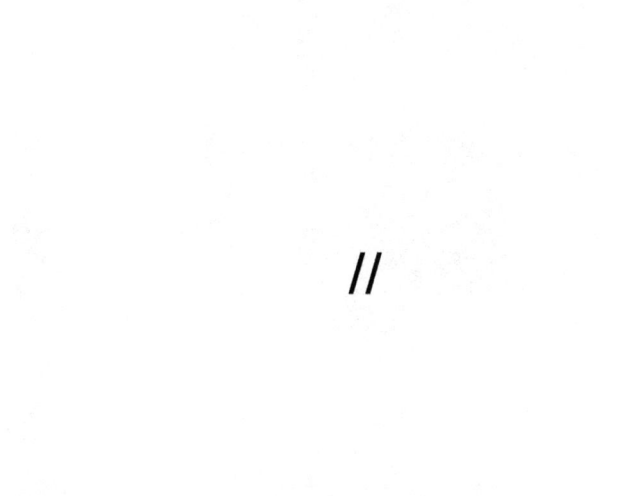

JANUARY 1ST

In the morning
I clean my son's
bedroom deliberately,
with special care
in the corners.

I will not let the dust
his body shed
last year
follow him
into this one.

WHILE MY HUSBAND WRITES OUR WILLS,
I PREPARE SUPPER

Shrimp take their revenge long after they have been
hauled up, reeling in the creel, long after they have been
beheaded and iced, long after they have been flown
across miles of verdant farmland, one grateful cow
tracing the jet's path across a cloudless sky.

The shucking is rote from years of practice:
plunge one hand into roe-clouded water,
flick down the legs, peel back the armor,
twist the bodymeat like a pencil in a sharpener
until I pull out the tail with a pop felt in my gut.

The whole process is so muscle memory,
so same-old-song-and-dance that I go gone
behind my eyes, no longer see the shrimp,
the sink, the neighbor's yard beyond my window,
sage fragrant in the summer air.

It is then each shrimp takes its revenge,
plunging a telson deep into the pad of my thumb,
bringing me back, suddenly, into the moment,
pulling me away from beneficiaries and bequests,
from guardians and executors,

demanding my apt attention
on this final flaying of a once living thing.

THREE GOLDEN SHOVELS FOR THE GRAVE

I

with thanks to Robert Hass

But the lamps are still lit, we
protest, the card table still ringed with die-
hard players dealing hand after hand as
though sunrise might break them even. If
we pour more drinks, there's a
chance the band will swing on, the ship
waltzing through water, our festivities its freight. And if we *were*
to get tired, why, that's not the end, we'd just be going
into the cabin to lie down
for a moment, just a moment. We'd merely be resting inside,
the party wrapping like swaddling waves around us.

II

with thanks to Jack Nicholson's Joker

I release the deep breath I've
been holding for seven years, been
biting my lips ragged to keep, dead
skin peeling and flaking. Once
surrendered, it hangs in the closet with the other things I've already
shelved: the baby clothes, the pills, the dream. It's
strange, now, the idea that a life other than this very
one could overtake me like some army that believes, as the city burns, that it
    is liberating.

III

with thanks to Crown Hill Cemetery

Experts advise against euphemisms like "gone"
or "passed" or "sleeping" which are too
likely to instill fear in a child. Soon

the questions will begin, that beloved
face turning to me as to the sun, more flower than child:

Do lilacs grow around the steps of her new home?
Who will she eat dinner with?
Where are you when you go to God?

And it used to seem that loving
was all it took to be a mother,

but now here is the rest,
breakfast dishes lingering on the table while we dive in
the deep end of metaphysics, never a moment of peace.

I want to stay faithful
to the truths I agreed on with his father,

yet some ache moves me to gather the bouquet of his face in
my hands, tip his chin to the velvet blue doming over us, to the
pinpricks that poke through the cloth. *There*, I say, *in the stars.*

PRAYER FOR THE DUDES WHO CATCALLED ME
IN FRONT OF MY TODDLER

after Lucille Clifton

I pray you reach your destination safely,
    but upon arriving realize that you have forgotten
    all the balloons for the douchebag parade.

I pray the other douchebags never forgive you.

I pray you get your heart broken by a mediocre white girl
    while your favorite song is playing.
    The joy the notes once conjured dissipates
    like her cucumber melon body mist.

I pray that the people with whom you are most open
    and vulnerable describe you as a friend
    of a friend.

I pray unending taint-itch through all your days.

I pray doctors care for you
    as lovingly and attentively as they do women in pain.

I pray rain, and the window of your car cracked just enough.

I pray two dollars in your account
    and two weeks until payday.

I pray crunch of dry ramen when the power company cuts the cord.

I pray your loved ones are alive, healthy,
    and disappointed in what you have made of yourself.

I pray all the porn videos you watch glitch right before the money shot.

I pray for you fear, hot and coppery.

I pray every time you step on an elevator
     you feel the bottom fall out from your stomach,
     that same startled alarm I saw in my son's eyes
     when he heard the doppler keen of your scream going by.

GROWING UP GOLEM

The golem's parents are at
their wit's end. They don't know
what to do with this creature
that woke up one day a stranger.
How carefully they once gathered
the clay, formed its limbs,
inscribed the sacred word
to place into its waiting mouth!
Now the golem stays out late,
dresses provocatively. It comes home
with smudged eyeliner,
smelling of mango vape smoke.
The golem's parents are attending
workshops, reading *From Emet to Met:*
Talking So Your Golem Will Listen,
Listening to What Your Golem Can't Say.
Still, the golem's failing classes,
ignoring teachers, breaking up
with a new boy every week
and cyberbullying all its exes.
The suspension slips pile up
like maple leaves in October.
The golem's parents enlist a therapist
and a tutor, a rabbi and a cool college student
from the Troubled Youth Mentor Center.
The golem flips them all the bird
and runs away for a whole weekend.
State troopers pull up with
the golem sniffling in the back seat.
It will not say where it's been.

While the golem curls up,
exhausted, under a patchwork quilt
of shirts it has outgrown, its parents
stand in the doorway, at the border of this
country to which they have no passports,
and have long forgotten the language.

FLOOD

My want, morning boy,
is to look beyond the end
of my own nose—beyond the bulb
of your head bobbing among
channel wrack and gutweed—
and see ocean musicking
itself against the coastline,
each wave a tone.

From the distance
of memory, morning boy,
I can edit the red-tide sludge
pinking the tide pools. I can love
the rocks the way water does,
lick by lick, wearing them pock-smooth
with my steady attention.

I had a flood of words,
morning boy. I tried to use them
to describe you, but you
drank them all down.

They're not sweet, you said,
they're not.

Stop crying, you said,
or I'll drink the tears too.

WHAT THERE IS TO LOSE

a golden shovel with thanks to Louise Glück

Leather shoes in the rain, of course, and the endless why
of your child's third year. A pillowy slice of cake. Love.
The demanding clamor of the five AM alarm that is what
drags you into each day you
would rather not face. The will
to live, sometimes. Try as you might to lose
the weight it will be there
to comfort you before bed, like a talisman under the skin. Is
there anything that stays, you will ask the stream of repo men, but they all
    say nothing.
Your closets and shelves overflow, no room for anything else
save the empty spaces where you used to
keep your vases, your best dress, your love.

WHEN THE WORLD IS TOO MUCH, YOU TURN
TO ONLINE LISTINGS

Walk into this breakfast nook: banquette set for one,
all cream walls and late morning lemon sun
puddling and dripping on the Restoration Hardware.
You could be the kind of person who uses the word "nook,"
who has time in their life to let the day age
with a cup of coffee, the kind of person
who probably knows personally the Sumatran farmer
who raised and roasted the beans in their hand-fired mug.

Or here, this dining room: black walnut trim,
broad French doors, tastefully framed advertisements
for Italian cafes. You could be the kind of person
who knows what risotto is and how to make it,
the kind of person who has capital-O Opinions on wine.
The kind of person who calls it BarTHelona
and has any number of former lovers in the region
to stay with on a spur-of-the-moment visit.

Or this backyard: lawn blending seamlessly into forest,
dappled light on the stream in the distance, cultivated wildness
of an English garden. Here you could be the kind of person
who spreads an antique quilt to read Tolstoy among the rosebushes,
the only person in book club who made it all the way through
the Very Important climate change book. The kind of person
who can do a rock-steady crow pose, who can actually
clear their mind when they meditate, a perfect blank slate.

None of the listings mention that you could purchase
any home as-is, turnkey ready, and it will still be you
who walks through the door when the sale has closed.

You, with your predawn alarm and booked weekends,
forgotten coffee gone cold. You, with your bottom-shelf wine
and penchant for burning everything you cook.
You, with your sexy vampire novels and cluttered mind,
no fantasy strong enough to fight the black hole pull of real life.

MAKEUP TUTORIAL

I have been a version of myself with less
grief to carry aback like the platter rocks
we would hump down trail, smoothing
the mucousy mess of the path after
spring rains blew through.

I have been a version of myself who thought
I had seen all grief had to offer, tasted
the buffet spread of long illness and overdose
and car crash and car crash. I didn't know then
about the griefs no grave can hold.

Online, I see children teaching other children
how to smudge and contour imitation dark circles
on the glass-smooth expanse between eye
and cheekbone. I follow the directions, step for step,
but in the end my face will not wipe clean.

small talk

his face a drain she can pour
her whole life down, on the margin as the party swirls

interlocking circles of family, acquaintances,
strangers making small talk under

boy-blue balloons, using paper plates
to quilt together a handful meal out of

single-finger foods, clots of
children in every corner, under every table,

lips red with punch like they dipped
lipsticks from the pile of purses on the guest beds,

all this eddying around the whirlpool of his face,
eyes blue-gray like the brackish water

on other side of the breakwall where she lost it,
her first and only time, all she could focus on

the rough jutting of the rock wall between
her shoulder blades, grating as the red

head he was pushing into her, brow furrowed,
hands on her shoulders as if bracing her for

the bad news that would come down months later
in the form of nausea, of breasts

more tender than old peaches, of a visit to
an aunt's house in the country, coming back empty

bra padded with cold romaine
that spills out like a story to a kind young man

who simply asked, what was it,
how does she know the birthday boy?

THE WAKE

a golden shovel with thanks to Robert Pinsky

Mourners array themselves around the room, disheveled. They
have not bothered with ties or jackets, no blouse met an iron. No one wants
    to tell
a priest not to speak well of the dead, but if it were me,
I'd break every fingernail on the gravedigger's shovel before going under
    cushioned on lies. The
tables have been pushed to the room's periphery, a whole world
of casseroles, hot dishes, starches. Here, the way we pay our respects is
to fill your mouth with all the things we said behind your back, a
divine act of transubstantiation, rancor unto funeral potatoes unto sorrow,
    like clock-
work. When he died, the widow clapped her hands, they say, said, "That's
that, then," and stood to begin her third act by winding
the bedsheets around him, her future out there somewhere, anywhere but
    down.

IN THE SMALL HOURS OF THE MORNING, I AM WEEPY
AT THE LUMINOUS THINGS OF THIS WORLD

On the empty street, a swallow has fallen
in love with my car.

It lives on the side mirror, offering a gift:
a river of shit down the passenger door.

The bean seeds in my garden drowse under the covers
of dark soil. They will doze five more minutes, maybe ten.

On the sidewalk, a dachshund runs
its tongue along the leash caught in its mouth.

My son's toenails need to be clipped.
Incorrigible, they will need to be clipped again come Sunday.

In the kitchen, a silverfish nestles in the arms
of the windowsill Madonna, six-legged savior.

What we have built here is spiderweb fragile,
the wind plucking each tethering thread.

Every feint and advance, every falter and rally
is another strand that wraps us in together,

we fragile animals, bird and bean and boy, dog and insect,
incandescent in the hours before sunrise.

ANOTHER LIFE

Public Works is deconstructing with mathematical precision
a massive maple that threatens the telephone lines, branches
leaning in to eavesdrop on million-dollar deals and petty gossip.
Men stand at the base, arrayed around a machine thrum-rumbling
with hungry insistence. Their eyes guide the loop that will steady
each branch for the saw, moving easily as a needle seeking thread.

My son watches from his perch in the bucket swing.
He gives equal attention to machine, loop, and saw,
to the limb that slips its binding and daggers earthward
toward one of the men, the young one who keeps tucking dark curls
under his hardhat only to have them escape time and again
like unruly children. The man dives out of the way just in time,
finding ground in a fountain of mulch.

There are seven alternate universes where the tree flourishes,
left to its own devices. Generations of children trying and failing
to reach its upper branches, dozing between cradling roots,
saying marriage vows in front of its broad trunk, leaves throwing
themselves from their branches in celebration.

There are twenty-three worlds where the man is fixed
like a showcase beetle to the earth, twelve others where
the bucket swing I push is empty. I wanted another life,
but this one has a dead stump, a living boy. This life holds me
like a loop around a tree limb, keeping me here in this world
where my son reaches up to be lifted from the swing,
where we go back together, my husband
spreading his maple-wide arms to welcome us home.

WHAT WE DO AFTER

When the word gets out that there is no God,
and the sky closes like a lid, we all go
on much the same as before. The old churches
continue to be converted into ramen lounges
and Spirit Halloweens, the most famous saints
still the ones with the glistening wet eggs
of Super Bowl rings perched above their knuckles.
We adjust to the way our prayers rebound, land
shuddering at our feet like stunned starlings.

We lived like there was no God
even when we thought there was one.
Now that we know better, we go out of our way
to avoid crushing the line of black ants
on the sidewalk doggedly ferrying
kernels of popcorn back to their hill. We keep extra
bandages in our pockets to give to the children
of strangers when they fall off their bikes.
The bandages have characters on them from the
cartoons we have continued to make even though
there is no God, cartoons where the frog and bear
say harsh words at first, then come together.
In the end, they share a blanket while they take
turns looking through their telescope
at the empty, star-filled sky.

ACKNOWLEDGMENTS

Thank you to the editors of the following journals where some of these poems first appeared, sometimes in earlier forms and / or with different titles:

82 Review: "Other People's Pregnancy Announcements"
Allium: "Flood," "They Tell Me I'm Gonna Be a Heartbreaker One Day"
Another Chicago Magazine: "January 1st"
Bicoastal Review: "Blighted Ovum"
Blanket Sea Press: "Born in the Rain" (as "Poem Beginning & Ending with My Birth"), "In the bower / the roses hang so heavy," "Self Portrait with Breast Pump," "Targeted," "Origin Stories," "The Death of the Dream," "In the Small Hours of the Morning I Am Weepy at the Luminous Things of This World" (as "The Year We All Planted Gardens")
B O D Y: "Growing Up Golem," "small talk"
Bottlecap Press: "Winter Awaiting Spring"
Cultural Daily: "Schoenbar Road," "Prayer for the Dudes Who Catcalled Me in Front of My Toddler"
Daily Drunk: Excerpt from "I Rewatch My Exes' Favorite Films and Imagine Our Lives Together"
Dead Letter Radio: "Targeted"
Drunk Monkeys: "When the World Is Too Much with You, You Turn to Online Listings"
en*gendered: "Venmo Request for Therapy Money from the Boy Who Called Me an "8" in His MySpace Hotness Rankings"
Flying Island Journal: "Between the Devil and the Clear Blue Sky"
Gastropoda: "While My Husband Writes Our Wills, I Prepare Supper"
Heavy Feather Magazine: Excerpt from "I Rewatch My Exes' Favorite Films and Imagine Our Lives Together"
Hog River Press: Excerpt from "I Rewatch My Exes' Favorite Films and Imagine Our Lives Together"

Lips: "I Ask My Therapist Where the Sadness Goes"
many worlds: "if i do not complete the thought you will never"
New York Quarterly: "The Wake"
Nexus Poets: "Bad Therapist Says"
ONE ART: "Estradiol the Mimic"
Portland Review: "At the Middle School Dance All the Boys Circle Up
    for the Crip Walk"
Querencia Press: "Pregnancy Tracker"
River Heron Review: "Three Golden Shovels for the Grave"
Sheila-na-gig: "Resume"
South Florida Poetry Journal: "What Arrives on Your Due Date," "What
    We Do After"
TAB: A Journal of Poetics: "What There Is to Lose"
Zoeglossia: "Another Life"

NOTES

The Bill Withers quote on page 17 comes from the album *Bill Withers Live at Carnegie Hall*.

The phrase "everything not saved will be lost" is a popular modification of the save progress prompt that appeared on some Nintendo consoles.

The line, "It was just that time of summer where your life smarts and itches" on page 52 comes from the Louise Erdrich novel, *Love Medicine*."

Erasures in this collection were created from the following source texts:

Jarman, Derek, et al. *Blue*. Artificial Eye; Distributed by World Cinema
    Ltd., 2007.
King, Stephen, et al. *The Colorado Kid*. Titan Books, a Division of Titan
    Publishing Group Ltd, 2019.
Kingsolver, Barbara. *The Poisonwood Bible*. HarperCollins, 1999.

Star Wars: The Empire Strikes Back. Produced by Gary Kurtz, directed by Irvin Kershner, performed by Mark Hamill, et al., Twentieth Century Fox, 1980.

THANKS

Thanks to Courtney LeBlanc for seeing the potential in this pile of poems, and for turning them into a real book. Thanks as well to Bianca Dagostino and to Kirsten Birst for their contributions in this process.

Real writing is a work of community. Thank you to Joan Kwon Glass, whose feedback on the earliest drafts of this manuscript have been essential to its success. Thank you to the Thursday night poets: Robert, Bethany, Alex, Stefanie, Rori, and Tim, who helped shape many of these poems.

I owe this life to so many people:

Thank you to my parents, Nell and Ed Klein, who gave me my literal life and then filled it with joy, support, and a deep love of reading. Thanks to my brothers, William, David, and Charlie, who were my first (and still best) friends. To Sarah, Caroline and baby Arnie, who have enriched our family beyond words. Thank you to my friends who have become family: Julia, Katie, and Marissa. Thank you to Jayne, Kevin, and the whole Kmitta family for welcoming me into your family, and for treating me like the true favorite son-in-law. Endless thanks to my husband Kris for reading every word of every draft of every poem in this book. Thank you for helping me clear off the kitchen table so I could cover it with manuscript pages. Thank you for listening to me endlessly debate word choice and sound, and for being right most of the time. You held me up when everything else was falling down. Your love makes this life worth it. Thank you to my son, Paul, who is both the heart of this book, and my heart living outside my body. I love you, Poppyseed.

I want to give special thanks to my undergraduate thesis advisor, Dr. Herman Asarnow. You read those first tentative, terrible, teenage poems, and you worked with me anyway. Because of your patience, honesty, and generosity, this book is possible. I don't know what a life without poetry would be like, and thanks to you, I don't have to.

ABOUT THE AUTHOR

Frances Klein is an Alaskan poet and teacher. Klein is the author of several poetry chapbooks, including *The Best Secret* (Bottlecap Press, 2021), *New and Permanent* (Blanket Sea Press, 2021), and *(Text) Messages from the Angel Gabriel* (Gnashing Teeth Press, 2024). *Another Life* is her first full-length collection. Klein's writing has appeared in *Best Microfictions*, the *Harvard Advocate*, the *London Magazine*, *HAD*, and others. She lives in Southeast Alaska with her husband and son.

ABOUT THE PRESS

Riot in Your Throat is an independent press that
publishes fierce, feminist poetry.

Support independent authors, artists, and presses.

Visit us online:
www.riotinyourthroat.com

RIOT IN YOUR THROAT BOOKS

Sarah Beddow   *Dispatches from Frontier Schools*

Kathryn Bratt-Pfotenhauer   *Bad Animal*

Kimberly Casey   *Where the Water Begins*

Sonia Greenfield   *All Possible Histories*

Brett Elizabeth Jenkins   *Brilliant Little Body*

Melissa Fite Johnson   *Green*

Melissa Fite Johnson   *Midlife Abecedarian*

Hadley Jones   *Devout*

Hilary King   *Stitched on Me*

Frances Klein   *Another Life*

Courtney LeBlanc   *Exquisite Bloody, Beating Heart*

Shilo Niziolek   *Little Deaths*

Laura Passin   *Borrowing Your Body*

Sara Quinn Rivara   *Little Beast*

Laurie Rachkus Uttich   *Somewhere, a Woman
Lowers the Hem of Her Skirt*

Karen J Weyant   *Avoiding the Rapture*